All about...

Rob Childs

Shaun McCarthy

www.heinemann.co.uk/library
Visit our website to find out more information about **Heinemann Library** books.

To order:
 Phone 44 (0) 1865 888066
 Send a fax to 44 (0) 1865 314091
Visit the Heinemann Bookshop at www.heinemann.co.uk/library to browse our catalogue and order online.

First published in Great Britain by Heinemann Library, Halley Court, Jordan Hill, Oxford OX2 8EJ, part of Harcourt Education. Heinemann is a registered trademark of Harcourt Education Ltd.

Editorial: Lucy Thunder and Helen Cannons
Design: David Poole and Geoff Ward
Picture Research: Rebecca Sodergren and Kay Altwegg
Production: Edward Moore

Originated by Repro Multi-Warna
Printed and bound in ROTHERHAM LIBRARY & Printing Company INFORMATION SERVICES
The paper used to print this book comes from sustainable resources.

ISBN 0 431 17986 7
08 07 06 05 04
10 9 8 7 6 5 4 3 2 1

J 823. 9

5 2 0 0 1 2 4 6 8

O€S 4580 82

British Library Cataloguing in Publication Data
McCarthy, Shaun
All about Rob Childs
823.9'14
A full catalogue record for this book is available from the British Library.

Acknowledgements
The Publishers would like to thank the following for permission to reproduce photographs:
Blackie / Bob Harvey / Chris Patton p**14**; Bridgeman Art Library p**21**; Rob Childs pp**4**, **5**, **7**, **8**, **10**, **11**, **12**, **15**, **16**, **17**, **22**, **23**, **24**, **26**, **28**, **29**; Kam Dhinsa / Manor High School p**19**; Frith Photos p**6**; Ginn p**20**; David Kearney, 1999 from *Time Rangers: A Band on the Run* by Rob Childs. All rights reserved. Repro by permission of Scolastics Ltd p**18**; Aidan Potts / Corgi Press p**25**; Raymonds Press p**9**.

Cover photograph of a publicity shot of Rob Childs, reproduced with permission of Rob Childs.

Sources
The author and Publishers gratefully acknowledge the publications which were used for research and as written sources for this book:

Authorzone magazine, issue 4, Sept 2002 **14**, **27**

Fiction works by Rob Childs are cited in the text.

Every effort has been made to contact copyright holders of any material reproduced in this book. Any omissions will be rectified in subsequent printings if notice is given to the Publishers.

Disclaimer
All the Internet addresses (URLs) given in this book were valid at the time of going to press. However, due to the dynamic nature of the Internet, some addresses may have changed, or sites may have changed or ceased to exist since publication. While the author and Publisher regret any inconvenience this may cause readers, no responsibility for any such changes can be accepted by either the author or the Publisher.

Contents

Any words appearing in the text in bold, **like this**, are explained in the glossary.

The author and Publishers would like to thank Rob Childs for his invaluable help in the writing of this book.

Who is Rob Childs?

Rob Childs is the king of sports stories for young people, especially football stories. He has written over 70 books. Around 50 of these are about football, such as the *Big Match* series of 18 books. But his stories are so good that they do not just appeal to football enthusiasts. Rob has also written non-football books based on ideas and characters from history. Guy Fawkes, for example, is of special interest to him.

Football or cricket?

As you can imagine, Rob is very keen on football himself! Before becoming a full-time writer he was a teacher for 20 years. Running school football teams was the best bit of the job for him.

▲ Rob has written over 70 books. Here are his first six sports books.

Rob has a terrible confession for a man who has written so many successful stories about football – he says he would now rather watch a game of cricket than a football match! He played cricket in the street and the park when he was a young boy.

His first book was *Soccer at Sandford*, **published** in 1980, about an imaginary school football team. He then wrote a book about athletics and one about cricket, but his football stories were so popular that he concentrated on new adventures for his soccer-playing characters. Readers just can not get enough of his football stories!

▲ Rob Childs, the teacher turned writer.

Factfile

★ Date of birth	3 November 1950
★ Star sign	Scorpio
★ Eye colour	Sort of greeny-grey
★ Hair colour	(What's left of it!) brownish with a greying beard
★ Pets	A rough collie dog called Rocky
★ Hobbies	Writing! Plus crosswords, cooking, book collecting and dog walking.
★ Favourite food	I love cooking – and eating – sausages and mash
★ Favourite childhood book	*The Hobbit* by J. R. R. Tolkien
★ Bad habit	Will admit to supporting Derby County, the Rams!
★ Personal motto	'Do it now! (Well, maybe tomorrow…)'

Football in the streets

Rob was born in Derby in the English Midlands in 1950. His family lived in Merchant Street on the outskirts of the town. It was an ordinary street of **Victorian** terraced houses. His father worked for Rolls Royce, the biggest manufacturer in the city, where he was an electrical engineer. In his spare time he played in several local football teams, so football was already in the Childs family. Rob's mother was a nurse in a Derby maternity hospital – where Rob was born.

Rob's grandparents lived next door. They ran a newsagent's. Rob remembers that he was he 'was never short of comics to read!'

▲ Derby, where Rob spent his early years. This picture was taken in about 1955.

Places to play

The area around Merchant Street was great for a sports-mad child to find places to play. Rob grew up in a time before streets were jammed with traffic and parked cars, so he and his friends could play football in the streets. Round the corner from his house was a quiet street beside a big factory. There was a drainpipe on the factory wall that made a perfect wicket for games of street cricket. Nearby was a recreation ground (known to local children as 'the recky') where football could be played on the grass.

Although the houses in Merchant Street had quite small gardens, Rob's family had taken down the fence between their garden and Rob's grandparents' next door. This gave Rob and his young friends a bit more space to play cricket.

◀ Rob the little cowboy aged three.

Rob invents a complicated game of cricket!

Rob and a friend worked out a clever system of using buckets and garden tubs as fielders so they could play a game of cricket with only two people. They had a ball on elastic that came back every time you hit it with the bat, until it dropped into a bucket or tub. That meant you had been 'caught by a fielder' and were out!

Mad about sport

When he was five, Rob started at Ashgate Primary School, at the top of Merchant Street, where he lived. When he was eleven he went on to Bemrose Grammar School. He stayed there until he was eighteen, doing O levels (now GCSEs) and A levels. He enjoyed creative writing in English lessons. He says that in both his schools he was a quiet, hard-working sort of boy.

▲ Ashgate Juniors football team, 1961/62 season. Rob is the goalie on the back row, third in from the left.

Going to the match

The thing Rob remembers most about this time is playing and watching sports. He was in the school football and cricket teams. At Bemrose School Rob was goalkeeper in the football team. He enjoyed being a 'goalie' and often has goalkeepers as main characters in his stories. (One of his most popular books is called *All Goalies Are Crazy.*) He remembers being 'better at catching than kicking', so it is hardly surprising that this was his favourite position in the team.

▲ Supporters of Derby County on the terraces during the 1960s.

Rob started supporting Derby County, the local football team, when he was nine. He would go to matches with his father or an uncle. They would stand up on the terraces around the pitch – these were during the days before football grounds had seats for everyone.

Typing classes

Rob decided he would like to be a **journalist** when he left school. He hoped to write general news **articles** for newspapers then specialize in sports stories. A good skill for a journalist to have is touch typing (typing on a keyboard without having to look at the keys), so he did an evening class in typing. He was sixteen, and the only young man in a class of young women training to be secretaries! Rob says that touch typing 'has been a fantastic skill for me as a writer'.

Off to university

In 1969 Rob left school and went straight to Leicester University. Leicester is another Midlands city less than a hour away from Derby. Rob chose it as a place to study largely because it was near enough for him to nip back to watch his beloved Derby County whenever they were playing at home!

Work and play

Rob spent three years at university studying **social sciences**. He says that going to university was as much about making personal changes as getting a good qualification. He remembers making a definite decision to change himself and the way other people saw him. No one else from his school went to Leicester with him.

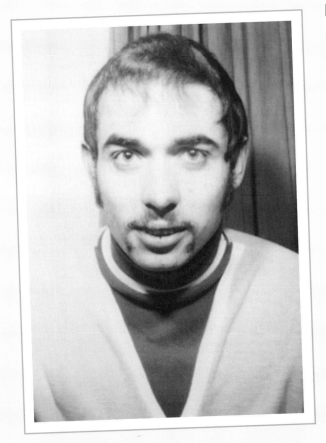

He lived in halls of residence with other students who were away from home for the first time, so he could start afresh at university with new friends. From being a quiet boy at school he became much more outgoing. He enjoyed going out and meeting people.

Rob's friends thought his new moustache made him look like a Mexican, so they nicknamed him 'Gringo'.

A new nickname

Rob went trekking in Morocco (in North Africa) during one university summer holiday. As part of his new image, he grew a long 'Mexican-style' moustache while he was away. When he came back to university his friends nicknamed him 'Gringo'. ('Gringo' is a Mexican nickname for Americans and Europeans.)

Rob still wanted to be a journalist, and he worked on the university newspaper, *Ripple*. He wrote all sorts of **articles**. He once spent all night on Leicester railway station so he could write a story about what happened there overnight.

'Gringo' falls in love

Perhaps the most important thing that happened to Rob while he was at university was that he met a student called Joy. They met at a Valentine's Day disco in 1971. Rob says jokingly, 'It was probably too dark for her to see what I looked like till it was too late!' Joy was studying sociology, a subject quite similar to Rob's social sciences, so they had interests in common.

Rob with Joy at a student ▶ dance in 1972.

'Plan B'

Rob passed his final examination, his degree, in 1972. He and Joy were married soon after they left university and decided to stay in Leicester. Joy got a job working for the Leicester University Press in their offices. In her spare time she wrote **articles** on historical subjects for magazines and newspapers.

Rob was interviewed for a job as a reporter on the local newspaper, the Leicester Mercury. It was his first step towards becoming a **journalist**. But he did not get the job. It was a big shock, and the end of his attempts to be a newspaper writer.

▲ Rob as a young teacher with his first trophy-winning soccer team.

This is how Rob describes his first teaching job:

'Getting up early to drive off to school after the lazy student days was a shock! I hadn't enjoyed cross-country running when I was a pupil at school, but now I found myself on the other side of the fence, taking PE lessons. I remember saying 'Right, lads, nice frosty morning – fancy a spot of cross-country?'

Plan B!

Rob had what he called 'plan B'. He would become a primary school teacher. He spent another year as a student, this time at Clifton College in Nottingham, training to be a teacher.

In 1973 Rob started his first teaching job in a middle school (for children aged ten to fourteen) in Loughborough, a town in Leicestershire. He still supported Derby County and wanted to be near enough to their ground to watch home matches!

Rob enjoyed teaching. He especially liked organizing the school sports teams. Five-a-side football was a favourite and his school team became very good. But he did not feel he was doing what he really wanted to do – writing.

First stories

It was at this time that Rob started writing his first short stories. These were stories for adults, not children. He wrote in the evenings after teaching. He especially liked writing stories with a twist at the end. Some of the stories were about sport. He sent them out to various newspapers, magazines and radio stations, and some were **published** or **broadcast**.

The big writing break

Rob left his first teaching job after a year and moved to Kibworth Primary in 1974. It was a friendly village school, again in Leicestershire. He was soon running the school's sports teams. His football squad was very successful.

After a year or two of teaching at Kibworth, Rob found himself writing his first stories for young people. He wrote about all sorts of things, including sport, but he was still writing just in his spare time.

The big idea

One day Joy said she had an idea: Rob should concentrate on writing stories about sports. Many young people loved playing and watching football and cricket but there were very few stories

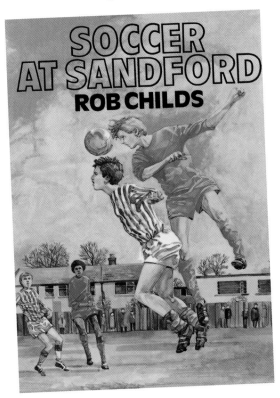

about sport for them to read. Joy suggested Rob have a go at writing a book-length football story for children, using his experience of running school teams.

So in 1979 Rob began writing *Soccer at Sandford*. When it was finished he sent it to several children's book **publishers**, and waited anxiously for their replies.

▲ *Soccer at Sandford*, Rob's first book, was published in 1980.

A most important letter

Then a letter from a publishers called Blackie's arrived. They wanted to publish Rob's book! Joy opened the letter, as Rob had left for school. She had to wait until the school's morning break before she could ring and tell Rob the great news.

After Joy's call, Rob says he walked into the staff room in a daze. When the head teacher found out, he told Rob how good this would look on application forms for teaching jobs. Rob says, 'I didn't have the heart to tell him that what I really, really wanted to be was a writer! Teaching just paid the bills ... Me and my class didn't get much more work done that day.'

▲ Rob the happy author at last!

More books, please

Soccer at Sandford came out in 1980, and it sold well. Blackie's wanted more sports stories from Rob so he continued to write. But he was still teaching during the day, and could only write in the evenings and in the holidays.

He used the same settings and many of the same characters in his next sports-based story, *Sandford On The Run*. This was about athletics, so he was able to introduce female characters. In the early 1980s very few girls played football at school and a story about them in a soccer team would have seemed a bit odd to his readers.

Rob used Sandford, his imaginary school, in more stories: *Sandford In To Bat*, about cricket, and *Sandford On Tour*, about football again. While he enjoyed covering other sports, football was the sport that Rob most liked to write about and that his readers wanted new stories about.

▲ *The Big Match* was Rob's first book with Transworld publishers.

1987 – a good year

Despite the publication of more books in the *Sandford* series of stories, Rob's writing still was not earning enough money to pay the bills. Then, in 1987, the publisher Transworld published his football story *The Big Match* in paperback. Rob saw this as a sign of better things to come, and decided to take the daring decision to give up teaching, to allow him more time for writing.

Transworld went on to publish lots of his books for many years. *The Big Match* was the start of a series featuring the same main characters that now runs to eighteen books!

Joy also had success with her writing in 1987. She had been writing **articles**, mostly about history, in her spare time. In 1984 she had had a romantic novel published. Now her first non-fiction book, *A History of Derbyshire*, was published.

▲ Rob in his back garden in Oadby, Leicestershire – with a football!

Pencils, pens and typewriters

In the early 1980s few people owned computers. Rob would write his first draft of a story out in pencil. Then he rewrote it in pen, then he typed out a third draft. He says 'Writing the first draft in pencil slowed you down and made you think. I did the second draft in ink so I knew which draft was which. Nobody gets it right first time.'

What Rob says

Although Rob was spending more and more time at home, writing, he had a very good reason to go out:

'My grandad always had dogs that would trail around behind him on his daily paper rounds. I'd always wanted a collie dog of my own to take for walks. They're so beautiful and intelligent. When we were first married Joy and I lived in a flat, but as soon as we bought a house, we got a little collie pup called Shane, who was born in 1979. The collie dog we now have is Rocky. He certainly thinks he's boss! I take Rocky for a walk every day, no matter what I'm writing.'

New books and old books

Rob was now a **full-time** writer, but *The Big Match* had only just come out and he needed some other means of making money. He and Joy decided to work together buying and selling rare old books. They would not run a bookshop but would search hard to find books specially asked for by collectors.

Unfortunately the business did not come to much, though for several years Rob and Joy bought and sold books they found at book fairs they visited. So Rob went back to doing a few days of supply teaching each week in local schools. He says, 'I still love browsing round cluttered old bookshops, though.'

▲ An illustration from *A Band On The Run*, one of the *Time Rangers* series of books.

A teacher again

Despite having several more titles in the *Big Match* series and other football books published, Rob found he needed to take another full-time teaching job in 1990. He and Joy were now living in Oadby, on the outskirts of Leicester. Rob got a job at nearby Manor High School.

▲ Manor High School, where Rob went back to teaching in 1990.

Every year of the 1990s more books were published. Rob started the *Time Rangers'* series, about a football team who travel back through time, having adventures and playing football matches! He also wrote some sports books for younger readers. After a while he went back to just teaching **part-time**, so he had time to do more writing.

From goalies to Guy Fawkes

By the mid 1990s Rob's **publishers** wanted him to write more and more football stories. Readers could not get enough of them. They knew how Rob could bring the tension and excitement of a real game to his stories. A young reader captured this feeling in a **review** he wrote of *The Big Match*: 'A dream comes true for Chris Weston when he's picked to stand in for the school team's regular goalie for a vital cup game. Will he cope with the team captain's taunts, will the match take place, or is the pitch water-logged? You can't wait to know what will happen.'

Time Rangers was now an eleven-book series of stories. Other new books included *Soccer Mad*, *Football Daft*, *Football Flukes*, *Football Fanatic* and *Soccer Stars*. Then Rob started the *County Cup* series of stories.

▲ *Gurgle the Goldfish* was inspired by a fish in a shopping bag!

Rob explains how ideas for stories can be found anywhere:

'Once, I'd been to the pet shop and bought lots of tins and bags of dog food. When I unpacked, I found a squashy plastic bag full of water at the bottom. There was a goldfish inside. The bag had not broken and the fish was unharmed. I took it back. It must have been put in my bag by accident. That fish became Gurgle the Goldfish in a story I wrote for young readers.'

The Gunpowder Plot

Rob does have other writing interests besides sport. Like Joy, he is interested in history. He wrote a book about the 16th-century sea captain Francis Drake.

Rob is particularly interested in Guy Fawkes and the other men who tried to blow up the Houses of Parliament – in the 'Gunpowder Plot' – on 5 November 1605. Rob has written two books about Guy Fawkes and what happened. Rob says he feels sympathy for Fawkes, who was betrayed, captured, tortured and executed. 'He was caught red-handed. It's like a detective story: no one knows who gave the plot away. It's a romantic, desperate story.'

▲ This is a 17th-century drawing of the men who took part in the Gunpowder Plot. Guy Fawkes is third person from the right.

A writer's life

Rob enjoys making visits to schools and libraries, meeting his readers. He signs copies of books for his fans who like to meet 'the face behind the books'.

How to write a good story

Often when he goes into a school Rob shows groups how he goes about writing a story. He brings lots of things to inspire young writers. He shows them his first notes for ideas for a story, then early drafts of the whole book, the artists' sketches for the illustrations: even the printers' proofs, which an author gets when the book is just about to be printed to give them a last chance to check for mistakes.

▲ Rob enjoys school visits, like this one.

What Rob says

Rob describes what it was like to be both a teacher and a writer:

'When I was doing part-time teaching and publishing books, I would be asked to do school visits as a writer. Sometimes I would be "Mr Childs, sir" in my own school in the morning, then "Rob Childs the writer" at a school visit in the afternoon. I liked it that way round. Coming back to teach at my own school after being treated like a star was a bit of a come down!'

Working for others

In 1994 Rob finally gave up teaching at Manor School to write. He also got involved in helping people with **dyslexia**. He had become interested in this when teaching at Manor School. Rob did a year's training with the Dyslexia Institute so he could teach children and adults who had the condition.

Although he liked helping people in this way, his **publishers** wanted more stories. He decided to give up working for the Institute to concentrate on writing, but he says 'I still do my bit for the cause by sometimes having dyslexic characters in my books and showing them in a positive light'.

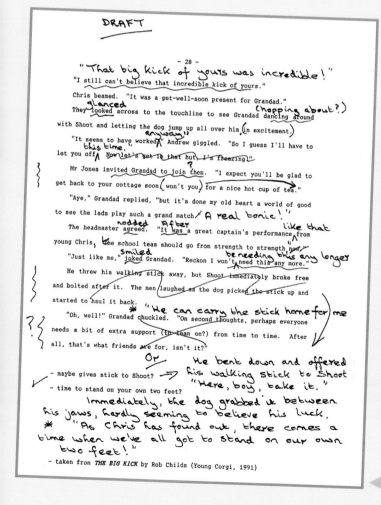

This is a rough **draft** of one of Rob's stories. It shows the hard work that goes into making one of his books.

A working day

In 2002 Rob and Joy moved to a new house near Leicester. Rob writes upstairs in a room lined with shelves of books. On other parts of the walls are displays of the covers from many of his best-known books.

Rob admits he is not 'a morning person'. He does not do much writing before lunch, but gets down to 'serious writing' in the afternoon. If the ideas are flowing he will work on in the evening or sometimes very late into the night. He says, 'It's not easy combining late nights with collie dogs demanding early morning walks. Sometimes I work into the wee small hours, have a dawn ramble with the dog – and then go to bed in the morning!'

Excuses, excuses!

Rob says that he finds all sorts of excuses to put off actually sitting down and getting started. But once he starts and gets involved with the story and his characters he works on and on. He writes quickly, straight on to a computer. He takes breaks from the writing to play computer games!

▲ Once Rob really gets down to writing a story, he just goes on and on, sometimes working all night.

Most of Rob's books have illustrations, and some of his working day is spent checking them to make sure they add interest to the stories they go with.

All in a day's work

As well as writing the stories, Rob has to do research, especially when he writes about history. He enjoys reading about the subjects he is going to write about.

Most days there are other 'writing' things to attend to: checking proofs (the final version of a book before it is printed), and looking at artwork for new books. Often Rob has to ring publishers and his **agent**. There are visits to schools to arrange, and letters from readers to answer. It's quite a busy life!

Robin Hood

For the *Time Rangers* series, Rob had to do historical research to get details right. In this extract from one book in the series, *A Band on the Run*, Robin Hood makes an appearance:

'The team were grateful for Robin's offer to share his outlaw's food cooked over an open fire.

"Not bad," said Dazza, "I could get used to this."

"You realise that eating the king's deer makes us outlaws as well," said Worm, "it's a hanging offence!"'

Rob Childs on Rob Childs

Here are some of Rob's answers to questions we asked him:

Do you enjoy schools visits?
'Yes. It must be hard for writers who have no experience of teaching to go into schools. When I go in, I feel at home. I don't just talk about myself. I do things that will show children how books are written and how they can do their own creative writing. Usually I come home dying to get back to my own writing!'

What do you do when you're not writing?
'Lots of things! I enjoy cooking, reading, and watching a bit of TV – mostly comedy and sport. I play snooker. I belong to a local snooker club. I don't really go and watch Derby County much any more I'm afraid. I enjoy photography and have taken some of the photos Joy uses in her history book and articles.'

Rob even does a spot of washing dishes in his spare time! ▶

What things do you not like?
'I don't like spiders or the sound of bagpipes – and I especially don't like spiders playing bagpipes.'

Where do your ideas come from?
'Usually they come from the characters I am writing about. Characters become like old friends, especially if – like the brothers Andrew and Chris, and their Grandad, in the *Big Match* series – they appear in more than one story. You follow where the characters lead. Sometimes, when you work this way, you get ideas for how the story can develop that you would never think of if you planned it all out beforehand.'

Of all your books, which is your favourite?
'That's a tough one. Maybe *Soccer at Sandford*, as that was my first success, or perhaps *The Big Match*, the first title in such a long-running series, or maybe one of the *Time Rangers* tales about the time-travelling young footballers. They were fun to write and research, combining my interests in history, **science fiction**, football and writing.'

Writing from experience

Readers like Rob's books because he creates such believable young characters. This is because he remembers playing sport at school himself. Rob says one of his best memories is of 'opening the batting in the annual cricket match against the staff and driving my very first ball for four off the seriously fast bowling of a usually sarcastic teacher. I can still see the look of amazement on his face as I whacked the ball!'

The future – a new season!

Rob is a friendly man with a good sense of humour, who has worked hard at various things before becoming a **full-time** writer. It is important to him that people enjoy his books. He says 'One of my best moments was having a mother come up to me after I'd given a talk in a library and saying: "Thank you for making my son into a reader."'

Books and more books

Some of Rob's stories are now being **published** again in collections – three stories together in one big book. He has recently written a series of 'spooky' football stories, the *Phantom Football* series. He has also written a book made up of three stories all about the same match but told from the points of view of three different characters. His publishers are always coming to him suggesting ideas for new stories.

▲ Rob relaxing with Rocky, the collie dog he got from Collie Rescue.

The Big Finish

Rob is also planning a final *Big Match* title, which would bring the best-selling series of stories he started back in 1987 up to nineteen titles. The last story would be called *The Big Finish*. Rob says it would 'bring together all the loose ends of the whole series and round everything off.'

Rob is very cheerful and excited about the success of his writing. 'The books have all been great fun to write and I hope to keep on writing many more in the future. There are a lot more goals in me yet!'

▲ Rob at a publishers party given to celebrate the success of his books. The cake has a football pitch on top of it.

Rob's writing tip

Rob has this advice for people who want to become writers: 'Keep a diary. I do. It helps you develop a writing style. Sometimes it's a daily thing – sometimes there are gaps for months. But it always comes back. It gets you into the habit of writing.'

Timeline

1950 Rob is born in Derby

1969–72 Studies **social sciences** at Leicester University

1973 Marries Joy

Begins teaching, in a high school in Loughborough, Leicestershire

1974 Moves to Kibworth Primary in Leicestershire. Besides teaching, he runs the school's sports teams. Begins to write in his spare time.

1980 *Soccer at Sandford*, his first book, is **published**

1987 Gives up teaching when *The Big Match* is published

1990 Returns to teaching

1994–95 Does a year's training with the **Dyslexia** Institute

1997 Becomes a full-time writer again

Books by Rob Childs

Here are some books by Rob you might like to read:

Soccer At Sandford (Blackie's, 1980)
Rob's first book about a school soccer team.

The Big Match (Corgi, 1987)
A school football team's nail-biting struggle to reach 'the final'.

All Goalies are Crazy (Corgi, 1995)
Sanjay is the team 'goalie', but the captain thinks someone else should have a go. Sanjay must prove he is the best.

Time Rangers 1: A Shot in the Dark (Scholastic, 1997)
Tanfield Rangers are transported back in time.

County Cup 1: Cup Favourites (Corgi, 2000)
Four schools are competing for a place in the semi-finals of the County Cup – and everyone wants to win.

Glossary

agent someone paid to do the business side of an author's work

article piece of writing published in a newspaper or magazine

broadcast TV or radio programme

draft first version of a piece of writing

dyslexia a condition that causes people to have trouble reading and writing

full-time a job done all the time (a full working week) rather than part-time

journalist person who writes for newspapers and magazines

part-time a job done for part of the week (either several hours a day or several days a week) rather than full-time

publish to produce and sell books. A company that publishes books is called a publisher. A published writer is one whose books are sold in shops.

review written personal opinion about a book, film or other public entertainment

science fiction a type of story-writing, usually about future or fantasy worlds, or set in space, using ideas from science and technology

social sciences the study of how people live together in societies

trekking walking long distances, usually in wild country

Victorian belonging to the time when Queen Victoria was queen (1837–1901)

Index

Titles in the *All About Authors* series are:

Hardback   0 431 17982 4

Hardback   0 431 17986 7

Hardback   0 431 17981 6

Hardback   0 431 17987 5

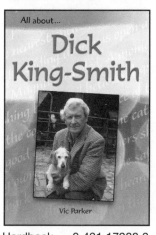

Hardback   0 431 17988 3

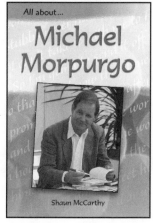

Hardback   0 431 17985 9

Hardback   0 431 17980 8

Hardback   0 431 17983 2

Find out about the other titles in this series on our website www.heinemann.co.uk/library